# How To Help Groups Make Decisions

By Grace Loucks Elliott

www.sunvillagepublications.com

Help Groups Make Decisions
By Grace Loucks Elliott

Copyright © 2011

No part of this publication may be reproduced, stored in a retrieval
system or transmitted in any form or by any means, electronic,
mechanical, photocopying, recording or otherwise, without prior written
permission from the publisher.

www.sunvillagepublications.com

Cover design by www.WebCopyAlchemy.com

## *table* of *contents*

**chapter 4**

The Chairman's Role in Helping
Groups Make Decisions     42

**chapter 5**

Special Methods in
Helping Groups Come to Decisions     59

## *introduction*

Sooner or later most of us become presidents, chairmen, or leaders of clubs, committees, boards, or other small units in the social, religious, educational, recreational, and civic activities that enroll a large proportion of the population in every community. These groups are forever faced with situations to work out, decisions to make that deal with an extraordinary variety of matters. An enormous amount of business is thus transacted. That is the way our common life is and that is the way we like it. Things would be very different, were we to do away with this great volume of grass-roots self-government.

### group decisions—everyone's business

When it turns out that these decisions have been made well, everyone is pleased, though the group members may not have been in full agreement when the decisions were made. Frequently the decisions prove to be wrong or unwise, even when the group has seemed to be in full agreement. When this happens, faith in democratic processes may be weakened. The remark that a camel is a horse put together by a committee is not a very accurate judgment on group decisions in general, but it describes what happens too often. Fortunately, ways are known for helping groups to come to surer, wiser, sounder decisions. *How to Help Groups Make Decisions* is for the use of chairmen, presidents, discussion leaders who have this responsibility.

### Harrison Elliott, pioneer of the "group process"

Among the first to make careful observations of how groups make decisions was Harrison Elliott. His great faith in the objectives and ways of democracy, and his belief that ordinary persons had not only the right but the ability to direct their own affairs did not blind him to the fact that their efforts often involve much bungling and lost motion. This he sought to correct, making experiments, refining his methods, developing his theories in a wide variety of situations—among students, among leaders of youth organizations, in the work of YMCA's, churches, and schools, in conventions where—until he pioneered new ways of working in small groups—everything centered around platform addresses.

To Harrison Elliott, democracy meant the participation of every person, in proportion to his ability, in the process of arriving at decisions. This gave a new meaning to the small face-to-face group, for it was there that individuals, otherwise lost in the crowd, found their place. He identified and described the phases through which discussion passed from problem to action. He clarified the role of the leader in the process. He believed that democracy, learned and practiced in small groups, could be ex-

8

tended into the larger activities of organizational, industrial, and civic life through the principles he developed and the persons who learned to use them. His book, *The Process of Group Thinking,* containing his philosophy and method, has been a classic in its field for many years.

Much of what we now do as a matter of course goes back to Elliott's observations on hundreds of groups that he led, or that were led by persons whom he trained. He pioneered the application of small group methods in the deliberations of large conventions of social, educational, and religious agencies. In recent years the scientific study of small groups and their leadership has produced much evidence that, in general, validates his faith in democracy and the correctness of his insights and methods.

**what this book is and is not**

This slighter book draws freely upon Elliott's work, and reflects to some extent these later developments. Several people, including myself, have collaborated with Mrs. Elliott to relate Harrison Elliott's insights to these later developments and new terminologies. It is not, however, a primer on group dynamics, nor a manual of sociometry, or of role playing, or of "buzz sessions," or of the social psychology of groups. Other books in this series provide introductions to these subjects.[1]

It is not meant primarily for "professional" workers, who in most cases have extensive resources at their finger tips. It is for volunteers, the thousands of men and women who, in the words of James Rietmulder, "help to keep the wheels going" in all kinds of settings, as presidents and committee chair-

[1] See "Suggested Reading" at end of book.

men, board and committee members, and leaders of groups, with special reference to youth agency, religious, social service, and related settings. There are tens of thousands of such persons who, often gladly, sometimes reluctantly, usually dutifully, undertake the leadership role in helping groups do things they want to do or have been asked to do—about programs, purposes, policies, plans, budgets, organizations, relationships, problems, recommendations, and all the other familiar tasks, which, added up, give us the things we do together in our common life.

Like anything else, the skill that chairmen and leaders of groups need, can be learned. A better grasp of the proved methods of working together will make it possible for them to help members of clubs, churches, social agencies, and citizens in the community, the nation, and the world to participate more intelligently and wholeheartedly in matters of concern to them and to society.

Let us see what is involved.

L. K. HALL

# 1

## *mainly about misconceptions and possibilities*

---

### groups are much like individuals

Just as there are individuals who act too quickly on impulse, so there are groups that respond too quickly to suggestion, doing whatever anyone may propose, without considering whether it is foolish or wise, unreasonable or sensible, useless or useful. Just as there are individuals who act entirely on authority, so there are groups that blindly follow orders. Sometimes this is wise and right, as in a crisis, when someone must take complete responsibility for what the group does. Usually, however, when a group blindly follows a leader, it is evidence that the group has not learned how to make decisions. Just as there are individuals who follow tradition, so there are groups in which tradition is the determining factor in action. Just as there are individuals who seem to be unable to make up their minds, so there are groups that are indecisive and futile in their thinking.

Good group thinking is a process that leads to reliable and convincing group decision, just as good individual thinking is a process that leads to reliable and convincing individual decision. With the right help, both individuals and groups can learn how to do it.

### not all group thinking is effective

Because thinking as a group means that its members share their thoughts, the process has both advantages and disadvantages over individual thinking. As each member makes his contribution, the thinking of other members is stimulated and modified. Under good leadership more points of view ordinarily lead to surer conclusions.

However, if the members of the group are badly led, or poorly informed, or inexperienced, or moved by strong prejudice, or for any other reason are not competent or disposed or able to think effectively, their efforts to come to decisions may be sheer waste of time, or, worse, they may come to very unwise decisions. Mob action is the extreme instance of this —a group doing things its individual members would not have the courage or perhaps even the inclination to do alone. Such results do not compare favorably with the thinking of an able and experienced individual, who, in his versatility, gathers up in himself more initiative, more data, more points of view, and better judgment about what is to be done, than do some groups.

The firmness and directness of authority, expressed in one-man leadership, cause many people to prefer to turn important decisions over to strong men whom they trust and willingly follow. There are often aggressive individuals, eager and ready to step into positions of power. In this book, we assume that democracy is the more desirable way of working in the large run, though we know there is no magic in the process. Experience has warned that attempts to be "democratic" in arriving at group decisions may not work out well, unless the right conditions are present. Good group thinking does not occur in a haphazard talkfest, or in a "bull session," where there is neither plan nor procedure and little information.

In the free-for-all of a "bull session" wit and ideas may sparkle, opinions may be shared, and the very irresponsibility of what is said and done may make it an occasion of interest and profit and enjoyment. There will never be a book on "more and better bull sessions," for their genius is in their spontaneity and freedom from rules and restraints. But the making of decisions is another matter entirely, and the chairman who permits his meeting to become a bull session when decisions need to be made is following a mistaken lead. Such a gathering wastes time, works in a circle, gets nowhere, and frequently ends in confusion. Valid decisions cannot be expected from such procedure. This is not democracy.

### democratic group conduct has to be learned

Independent, self-directing group conduct is an achievement. Merely to offer democracy to a group does not mean that the group will practice it. It has been shown, however, that once competence for it has been learned, the group gets more done, there is more satisfaction among the members, there is more growth in the kinds of ability, attitudes, and relationships needed in a democratic society. This is an important consideration.

Some chairmen see only two possibilities: either to take full control, or to keep hands off altogether. If the chairman does the one, the group does little thinking for itself; if he does the other, the discussion may be confused and profitless. In neither of these ways does a leader help the group to learn how to do good thinking. The duty of the chairman in a group unaccustomed to thinking together is to take whatever control of the discussion is necessary to secure a genuine consideration of the problem. This may mean assuming complete control, at first; but it should be control of the procedure of the group rather than dictation of its conclusions. It is important that the emphasis be on how to think, and not on what to think.

### sham democracy must be avoided

It is a travesty on democratic participation when a leader deliberately makes use of a democratic method in order to secure assent to a conclusion already fixed. A clever leader sometimes makes a group believe it is going its own way when it is actually being led to a prearranged decision. This may be sheer dishonesty, or, at best, it may be overzealous-ness. Only the most inexperienced persons fail to see through it. Consideration is given below to the ways in which a leader guides toward desired conclusions without violating democratic procedure.

### turning things over to those who are not responsible does not help

It sometimes seems that the process of democratic participation shifts responsibility to those who actually cannot discharge it well. Some assume that democracy means turning the conduct of the home over to the children, the factory to the working men, the school to the students. A camp director, wishing to be democratic, asked his staff to make certain discipline decisions for which no one but himself could be finally responsible. He soon found that it did not work, for to be fair to campers and parents he sometimes had to reverse decisions made by his less experienced staff. It would have been wiser to place the problem before his counselors, seeking their judgment as to what to do, but with the understanding that he must make the decision. In the same camp a council of campers were asked to make so many decisions about program that they finally asked, "What are the counselors for?"

As a matter of fact, this is not democracy, because although democracy means the participation of *all* who are involved in a situation, it must be in proportion to each one's ability, and, let it be added, to his *responsibility.*

Group thinking is not a process that turns ignorance into wisdom. A thousand contributions of misinformation and unreliable evidence do not add up to a reliable sum. There is need for the expert, for the well-informed person, and for dependable ways of getting information.

To help groups make decisions does not mean to reduce the level of thought to that of the less experienced, the less wise, the less competent, the less far-seeing. It does not eliminate the expert, the prophet, the "real leader." Left to themselves, the members of a committee may, in fact, ignore an expert who might help them greatly, or even reject one who, because he thinks faster and further than others in the group, might awaken them to a sense of purpose and far goals. This sort of thing happens frequently. In a group where all are working together, the gifted individual should find his greatest channel for usefulness.

Group thinking, then, relates the more able, the

more mature, with the less able and the less mature in a process that gives each a chance to share according to his ability. In terms of getting work done, in terms of helping persons grow, in terms of satisfaction to all, this is a creative situation.

### group thinking is different from argument

The method of argument and debate is usually not a profitable form of group thinking. In argument the persons on each side usually have their minds made up. The purpose is to convince or defeat their opponents. In genuine discussion there is respect for other points of view and a readiness to change one's mind on the basis of new light. Every chairman knows that this ideal is difficult to achieve. Individuals who have prejudged the question listen but do not readily change their minds. Their concern is to make their own ideas prevail. Aggressive and enthusiastic persons tend to sweep opposition before them. Less outspoken persons hesitate to resist them. Hypersensitive persons quickly become defensive.

### good group decision making requires certain conditions

Productive group thinking occurs only when the situation is characterized by the following elements:

*Involvement of the Members.* The ability of a group to come to a good decision is dependent, in the first place, on the involvement of the members with one another, on their recognition of common interests, and on their willingness to be related. In such a group the members who know that they have a specific contribution to make accept the chairman as one who can help them to participate effectively. Those who are less concerned about the issue under consideration will require more of the chairman's help before they become involved and willing to contribute as the discussion develops.

*Relation of the Problem or Decision to Responsible Action.* Any discussion is dynamic only if the question to be decided is one which is of real concern to the members of the group and one in relation to which they realize that they must take some action. Until there is this "readiness," discussion is academic and lacks reality, since the decision to be reached does not vitally affect those who are discussing it.

No discussion is sound when the issue has already been decided by organizational policy or statute and the group is misled into considering a question as if it were free to act when actually its decision will make no difference. The discussion of a group's attitude toward any policy, rule, or law established by someone else can be productive only if the discussion is related to what to do within the established rule or policy, or how the group might go about getting it changed. To work for a change in regulations or law calls for further discussion between those who question its soundness and those who have the authority to modify the *status quo*. It is always important for a leader or chairman to help his group understand the ground rules and the reasons for them. Groups usually can see the value of reasonable rules once they understand them.

*Difference in Point of View.* A third requirement is a real possibility for differences of opinion, values, or priorities within the group and opportunity for these differences to be faced by the members. Otherwise there is no question, for if thinking is to be truly creative, individuals must have enough respect for each other to be willing to clarify their differ-

**17**

ences rather than to gloss them over. Also, when there are additional relevant points of view which are not known to the group, someone should try to know these and present them as fairly as possible. If this is not done the decision may have to be reopened at a later time because essential data were not properly taken into account.

*Bonds Which Unite the Group Members.* Awareness of a common interest or concern binds the members together, engendering some of the patience necessary to reach a creative decision. To be held together requires something more cohesive than the special interests of a few or the factions around contending alternatives. Bonds must be great enough to bridge the differences of point of view and to make modification and integration possible. This bond may be the recognition that failure to find a solution may hurt the interests of all involved. It may be concern for the effectiveness of the organization to which the differing members belong and regarding whose task they have conviction. It may be the phrasing of its aim or purpose or consideration of differences of opinion about methods of carrying out that purpose clarifying or reinterpreting it. The bonds may appear as simple as a need for fun or companionship; or they may be as complex as the need for security and survival; but they must be there, and the members must be in some measure aware of them.

### this chapter closes with one brief reminder

Not all discussion leads to decisions, nor should it always do so. There are other reasons for discussions, but they are not included here. Conversely, not all decisions are made by the discussion method, nor should they all be. A group may decide certain things by voting, with little or no discussion; by delegating the decision to a committee, an officer, an adviser; by adopting some other group's plan; or by joining with some larger unit with an already established course of action.

The thesis of this material is that discussion is one of the most effective methods whereby a number of people can think through and come to a decision about something they have in common; that some kinds of decisions can be made in no other way; and that most of us would like to improve our decision-making techniques.

Few things are static, and decisions are inescapable. Good ones can make life more fun, more worthwhile and abundant. Good ones depend upon our learning how to reach them, but their roots go far deeper than method—they go to the sources of insight and commitment, the spiritual quality of the individual who, in taking part in the group, brings whatever he holds most dear and will work hardest to become and to achieve. The group process will mold him, but he also will mold the group; whatever we can do to enrich one will enrich the other. The leader's task is to evoke participation at these deeper levels whenever he can.

# 2

## *the groups* we *lead*

### kinds of groups

Whether one is called chairman, president, adviser, or leader may not matter very much, but he should know the *kind* of group for which he is responsible. Social scientists have found many useful ways of describing and classifying groups, but for our purposes we need think of them only in terms of the *kinds of decisions they can make.*

*Groups That Make Management Decisions.* Good examples are the board of directors of a social agency, the board of management of a YMCA branch, the standing committee of a church (standing committee here means the controlling body in a church, for which there are many names), the directors of a Community Chest, or the executive committee or board of a local nursing association. These groups provide technical, administrative, and policy decisions for their parent organizations. Almost always there is a constitution that states the responsibilities and authority of the groups in broad terms. They are usually "permanent" committees. If they are subordinate to an over-all controlling board they are governed by by-laws, or by a commission issued by the board of directors. In addition, they are bound to take into account the policies and standing rules previously adopted by themselves and their predecessors, as well as accepted ethical practice in dealing with professional employees. Within these broad limits they have independent "competence."

Because of the importance of the decisions they must make, parliamentary procedures are customary, and the vote of a majority is recognized as binding on the whole group. Careful records of actions are usually kept.

*Groups That Make Executive Decisions.* Illustrations are a committee appointed to select a contractor to erect a building; a committee that acts *ad interim* in behalf of a board; a committee appointed to plan a convention, or conduct an athletic contest, or a party. Such matters are referred "with power," as we say, to committees, but the decisions of such committees are strictly limited to the tasks which they have been appointed to carry out. The chairman's first task, then, is to help the committee understand exactly what it is asked to do, and beyond which it cannot go.

*Groups That Make Advisory Decisions.* Examples are commissions and committees appointed to study and make recommendations to the parent body on any matter: for example, a town planning commission; a research group that presents findings based on research or experiment; a nominating committee; a budget committee; an interorganization committee appointed to make recommendations about issues of conflict or areas of possible co-operation; department

21

committees, such as physical education department or youth department, that decide upon needed budgets, equipment, star!, policy and tie like, and present their recommendations to the board of directors; an intergroup council. These committees may be permanent or temporary.

Many such groups make both management and advisory decisions. This is true of most standing committees (and here the term standing is used in contrast to temporary or *ad hoc* committees) in educational, recreational, religious community agencies. Within the limits of their commissions, they are competent to decide *and act*. But awareness of *specific* responsibility, and *specific* authority is the first essential in the making of effective advisory decisions. A typical illustration of the limits on an advisory committee's decision is that of a committee appointed to find a minister for a church. It may investigate and interview candidates and come to a decision about whom to recommend, but without authorization from the church electorate it usually cannot issue a call.

*Groups That Are Self-Directing and Whose Decisions Mainly Concern Their Own Members and Their Own Activities.* Such groups are legion. Examples are the youth groups in social, religious, and educational organizations like the Christian Associations and the Scouts; many informal education groups; clubs of all kinds, some being quite independent, some being related to parent organizations; the League of Women Voters; the Parent-Teacher Association; the women's society in a church; a neighborhood council. These groups often have their own constitutions, even when they are units in parent organizations. Their decisions are related to their own purposes, programs, membership policies, codes of conduct, dress, in respect to which they usually have considerable freedom so long as they conform to what is expected of them as parts of larger organizations.

Such groups also very frequently engage in another kind of decision-making activity—that is, helping their members to come to individual decisions on questions relevant to their age, situation, ideals and the like. For instance, a young adult group may conduct discussions on interfaith marriage, a teen-age group on attitudes toward persons of other races, a League of Women Voters on election issues and candidates. Group decisions are usually not made in such cases, but the influence of the group in helping its members make good decisions may be very great, even though individual members may reach different conclusions.

### the difference it makes

For members to be well aware of what kind of groups they are helps them to know *what kinds of decisions they can or cannot make,* and, to some extent, helps them to know *how they should go about making decisions.* What is appropriate in one kind of group may be quite inappropriate in another. Many groups are not clear as to what kind of group they are. The first step in helping them is to make this clear. The chairman, adviser, or leader may have to go to the president or executive for the answer, and even they may not have it. There is nothing that blocks effective group decisions more than ambiguity about what is expected of a group, and what degree of freedom it has in doing it. Many organizations are not clear and consistent in their philosophy or their practice on this point.

The chances are that you have been chairman or adviser of several committees or groups. Below is a list. Where do you belong in it? Identify it as a management group, an advisory group, a self-directing club, or an executive group. Have you been clear as to the group's functions and limitations? Are the members clear as to their relationships, responsibilities, freedom of action? Have you been helping the group to use methods of making decisions that are appropriate to a group of its kind?

1. A Hi-Y or Y Teen club deciding on fall program
2. A high school council working out a code of dress for students
3. A League of Women Voters deciding on its pol icy in respect to issues in the next election
4. The standing committee of a church
5. A conference committee working on program, fees, speakers
6. A hearing group discussing a proposal being con sidered in a convention
7. An intergroup council in a social agency
8. A board of directors
9. The executive committee of the PTA
10. A committee in the local YMCA or YWCA
11. The local Boy Scout council
12. A Girl Scout troop
13. A young adult group in a church or Y
14. A 4-H club
15. A town planning commission
16. The budget committee of the Community Chest
17. A commission to study juvenile delinquency and recommend plans
18. A street corner gang

19. A cabin group at camp
20. A family
21. (Fill in your own)
22. _____
23. _____
24. _____
25. _____

# 3

*steps in coming to decisions*

---

In coming to a group decision that leads toward action there are four steps:

1. Seeing what the problem is
2. Considering possible alternatives
3. Reaching a conclusion
4. Moving toward action

In actual practice these steps are interrelated, and a group may work back and forth among them in its thinking. The separation into four steps is for analysis rather than to insist that they always follow in logical order, but each step is essential. Two illustrations follow, here greatly oversimplified:

### an illustration of teenage decision making

Fifteen teenage boys and girls came together in the home of two of them with a rather keen desire for "some sort of a club," but only vague notions of how to get it or what it would do. A young college graduate with some experience in group leadership had been asked to come and help them plan. Sitting in the circle with them he raised the question, "Why do you want a club?" The answers revealed their desire to have something to do; they wanted some fun; they wanted to belong to something. Some of the young people in the community had been getting into trouble. "We think if we had a club it might help prevent this sort of thing." A similar club had been organized two years before but it hadn't worked out very well and as its members grew older they dropped out. How could that be avoided with this new club? After a half-hour the leader, who had not taken an active part beyond keeping the discussion on the subject, said something like this: "As I see it, you feel the need for some organized recreation and fun. But if you have a club you want it to be successful. How can we get it? What would be its purpose? What kind of organization should it have? Who should join? What about leadership? What about program?" The group agreed to this statement. "All right," he said, "let's begin with the purpose." This led rather quickly to several suggestions: fun, friendship, learning how to conduct meetings, having some good ideals, and the like. These alternatives were seen not to be mutually exclusive, and they went to a somewhat deeper level than had been in the minds of the group members earlier in the evening.

So the discussion moved on into other phases of their problem. What they did about program was especially helpful as an illustration of the four steps in decision making. The problem, at first, was seen in terms of "no place to go," "no tennis courts," and the like. The leader said, "Let's see what you'd like, and then we will talk about what possibilities there are." This led to a free-wheeling half-hour in which suggestions followed in rapid succession, some of them obviously impractical. The leader made no negative comments, and kept the group from losing time in argument. "Let's get all the ideas we can, and then see where we are." The summary he presently made included all that had been mentioned, and he added a few more. To bring things to a conclusion, he then suggested that they do some short-range and long-range planning with their ideas. Quickly they decided on a meeting the next week in which they would talk about organization, then go to the movies to see a current film dealing with a serious social problem. Other meetings for this month, and what would be done in them were quickly planned. Two or three major events for the next month were spotted. A calendar of dates—Halloween, Thanksgiving, Christmas—was made up. A schedule of things they hoped to do—in fact, more items than any club could expect to cover in one season—was left on the long-range plans list. Finally, at the close of the meeting, responsibilities were assigned and accepted: a first draft of their constitution to be written; arrangements for transportation to the movie; an invitation to a speaker. The leader, knowing the need for follow-up, made dates with the individuals responsible for these duties for the purpose of seeing that no one forgot, or ran into difficulties beyond his ability.

The four steps in the decision-making process were easily visible to an onlooker in this two-hour session. The rather skillful leader did not dominate, or decide for the young people, but he maintained an "evocative" situation in which all participated, and the group ended up with a keen sense of accomplishment. Without his help, it might well have been little more than a bull session.

The general bodies of two national church de-nominations that were in process of merging ap-pointed a joint committee to draw up and submit to the churches a new statement of faith. In preparation for its first meeting the members of the committee were asked to read a number of the historic creeds of the Christian church. This "homework/' along with the rather explicit directive from the general committee of the uniting churches, provided a good orientation to the committee's problem. Nevertheless, it was necessary to spend considerable time in further exploration. What end was the statement to serve? Should it lean heavily on tradition in both style and content, or should it be forthrightly modern in both respects, or should it seek to combine the traditional and the contemporary? How was it to be used? A two-day session of the committee led to a clear-cut understanding of its task. In preparation for the second meeting all its members tried their hands at drafting a statement. These, when duplicated, became the workbook of the second session. In the wide range of content and style that appeared in the statements there was much agreement, which the chairman helped the group to recognize. Three or four of the statements seemed especially promising, and their authors were asked to develop them further in preparation for the third meeting. In the third meeting the merits of one of these was quickly seen, both in content and style. It was evident, moreover, that the thinking of every individual in the group had made its contribution, though the final product was well unified. The last act of the committee was to agree upon procedure in presenting the statement in the general synod of the uniting churches.

In this illustration also, the four steps of effective

**29**

decision are easily identified: seeing the problem, developing and evaluating alternatives, coming to a conclusion, moving toward action. As in the preceding illustration, the four steps are separated in logical analysis, though in some form or other all four were present most of the time. The chairman, in the second instance, was a seasoned veteran in committee work. It was clear that he sensed the nature of the committee's work at any given moment, and helped to maintain vital orderliness in the process.

### further analysis of group decision procedure

The reader, with the four steps in decision-making procedure in mind, will be thinking of other and more immediate illustrations in addition to those described. It will help him in making his analysis of the process, if he will bring to mind some group of which he is now chairman, president, or leader, and reflect upon recent decision-making activity. Let him identify in his own experience as many of the points in the following outline as possible:

AN OUTLINE OF GROUP DECISION PROCEDURE

1. *Seeing what the problem is*
   a. What is the situation? (What, who, why?)
   b. What factors in the situation are important and must be taken into account?
   c. What are the specific questions to be decided?
2. *Considering possible alternatives*
   a. Examination of possibilities:
      (1) To meet the situation and problem as out lined, what are the possible courses of action and the reason for each?
      (2) What bonds seem to unite the group? On what is there agreement in fact, principle, or objective?
      (3) What are the chief differences, if any (on

matters of fact, objectives, principles, desires)?
  b. Exploration of differences as to facts and points of view:
     (1) What additional information is needed? Hew can it be secured?
     (2) Can the differing points of view be talked out?
3. *Reaching a conclusion*
  a. What decision will best take into account the relevant factors, the purposes and desires of the group, the various points of view?
  b. What are the reasons for this decision?
4. *Moving toward action*
  a. What are the ways and means of putting the decision into effect?
  b. What are the next steps? Whose responsibility? (What, where, how?)

**how it works**

Let us look now at how a group, large or small, may be helped in carrying through this decision-making process:

*Getting the Situation, Its Central Problem, and Relevant Factors into the Open.* A question for discussion always represents a problem in a setting. In whatever form the problem faces the group it is not sufficient just to state it. Time must be taken to see what prompted it, who brought it up, and why. Time must be taken to learn how it appears to various members of the group. Each person not only must be aware of the problem as it appears and feels to him, but also must see how it looks to others in the group. The chairman does not know what the issue means to the members of the group, nor does any member of the group know what it means to the others, until there has been enough time to develop

**31**

this mutual understanding. As various persons emphasize different factors, the situation and its problems take on new meaning, and elements otherwise overlooked come into focus.

These important factors in the situation become the tests to apply to any solution the group will consider. Will the decision do what is wanted or needed?

Some of these factors will reflect likes and dislikes, the attitudes, prejudices, and oddities of the members of the group. Some will reveal the different situations in which the members find themselves. Some will reveal purposes, hopes, willingness. Some will reveal relationships between members in the group.

If the chairman is alert he will note in this opening part of the discussion where the difficulties in reaching a conclusion will probably be. He is likely to discover that some individuals are talkative, some are aggressive, some are thin-skinned, some are cooperative, some are surface skimmers, some are quiet, thoughtful, and clearheaded, but may not at first be very influential in the group. These personal observations lead him to see what possibilities there may be, who has the clearest ideas, what suggestions seem to strike fire, what conflicts of ideas and personality are likely to arise. Even at this very early stage, he will need to be on guard against his own tendency to like some persons in the group better than others, or to jump to conclusions about the problem and its solution.

A time comes in the preliminary discussion when no new contributions are being made. Then the chairman (or someone else whom he may have asked to do it) makes a summary in which are stated the problems, the important factors, the specific question or questions, to be answered. It is important to make the summary brief and clear, a springboard for the renewal of discussion. It should include points of agreement and of disagreement about the problem, not about its solution. Getting the issue clear is the vital first step. He may wish to say, "Let me see now if I can state where we are." As he completes his summary he may say, "Is that about right? Have I left out anything? All right—the question now before us is, . . . ." Above all, the summary should not be a rehash or a speech. Its purpose is to drive in the peg that marks a turning point between stating the problem and searching for the solution.

This first phase of the process is so important that it merits a few more words. Unless it is well developed, what follows it is not rooted in a good understanding of what is being talked about and why. Do not substitute a lengthy statement by the leader in place of it. Do not omit it by simply stating the question and asking at once for a decision. Chairmen may need to put the brakes on as members rush ahead and try for decisions before the problem has been fully broken open. The chairman may sometimes check the too-quick suggestion by saying: "That is a good suggestion. Can we hold it over for a little while as we try to state our problem?" He must then not forget to bring the point in at the proper place. The leader has no more important task than that of being aware, and helping the group to be aware, of the exact stage of the discussion in which it is working and of where it has led them.

Now we move on to how the leader helps the group in considering alternatives.

*Considering Alternatives.* The second stage in discussion is the examination of possible courses of action which seem to be real options for the group. The chairman must be sure to state the specific

**33**

question in relation to the summary just made, so that it will be evident that the discussion is now sharply focused, and not a general search for a general solution to a general problem.

Be sure to see that every option or proposal which seems important to members of the group is recognized and considered, even though it may not seem important to the chairman. Be sure also that any proposals that should be considered but which have not been mentioned in the group are brought forward in some way also.

In some cases, the options will be limited, by the nature of the situation, to going along with a proposal that has come to the group, or rejecting it, or working out some kind of compromise.

In any case, get all the proposals in front of the group before action is taken on any one. If a decision is made too soon on any option, before it is seen in relation to others, it may be necessary to turn back and take a new look at it. For this reason, the discussion should be kept fluid. The attempt to get consensus should wait until all the options and their pros and cons are in sight.

The reason for being sure that all the possible alternatives are before the group is fourfold. First, advantage should be taken of all possible ideas and experience. Second, to pass by suggestions made by individuals or minorities may leave them frustrated and unable to share wholeheartedly in discussion. Third, many decisions are integrations or compromises among options, and all should be weighed. And fourth, originality and creativity in a group grow out of richness rather than the leanness of experience and suggestion.

When each proposal is made, its reason may be given; or reasons may be given after all are listed.

It is quite important to hold up discussion of any particular course of action until all proposals are made and reasons for them given by those who made them. The leader may need to check quick judgment, and the tendency to get involved in arguments about proposals before the members have them all before them. Indeed, he may need to check his own inclination to question a proposal made by a group member.

The discussion of the proposals involves a prediction of the likely consequences, and a comparison of these consequences. The accuracy of the prediction and the desirability of the consequences must be considered. The chairman should help the group to avoid snap judgments. If the members are making seemingly wild claims for a proposal, the chairman may ask, "What are the reasons for thinking it will work out this way? What is the evidence?" Similar questions would tactfully challenge too-quick condemnation of a proposal. In asking such questions, however, care must be taken not to put individuals on the defensive. Avoid asking them why *they* think so and so, by asking why *people* think so and so. A way to remove prejudice, release emotion, and secure open-mindedness is to ask the group to look at the reasons why views to which they are in opposition are held by other persons. On one occasion when a group had split into two violently opposed factions the chairman used the radical device of stopping the discussion, then asking each member to give reasons why persons might honestly take a position opposite from his own. When individuals commence stating the good points in another position they have taken the first step toward creative compromise.

It is important to discover the purposes, points of emphasis, goals, on which the members of the group are united. These common desires or values are the bonds that hold the group together. There may be differing proposals for achieving their aims, but if there is agreement on what the aims are, there is a good climate for considering different proposals. When the chairman discovers that there are hidden and conflicting purposes not fully brought to light, he has a more difficult problem on his hands.

Uniting bonds are of several kinds. Sometimes it is loyalty to the organization or group and its welfare. Sometimes it is a common problem that concerns them all. Sometimes there are common ideals underlying all surface differences. Sometimes it is a common prejudice. Whatever the bond or bonds, the chairman should recognize them in his summary.

Differences as to facts and opinion should also be identified and stated in such a way as not to embarrass any individuals. These differences should be brought clearly into the open. No genuine compromise can occur by glossing them over as if they did not exist. If there is disagreement as to *fact,* appropriate steps must be taken to get reliable information. A committee discussing the need for a neighborhood swimming pool splits on its cost. The enthusiasts cite a figure that strikes the more conservative ones as ridiculously low, and they in turn talk figures extravagantly high. Obviously, expert help is needed to get this factor understood in terms of realities. Sometimes a group will need to join with another group in an actual experiment. It has been proposed, for instance, that a parents' group and a teenage group meet together to discuss teen-age standards of behavior. Some say, "It just won't work." The way to find out may be to try it and see.

Often the discussion turns upon a difference as to what is *desirable.* After all the facts are in, differences remain. The parents and teen-agers may have interesting discussions, but some may feel it did not improve matters and will not wish to repeat the experience, even though others will feel more joint meetings should be held.

It is the chairman's business to see that the agreements and differences are clearly faced. "We are agreed on these things," he says, "but on these other things we are not. In the face of these agreements and differences, what shall we do?" Someone may suggest a vote, and at times this is the way to proceed. The chairman must, however, find out from the group if there is willingness to abide by the results. A close vote may leave the group still divided. A small minority of influential persons may disturb the confidence of the majority in the vote they have taken. There is this to be said in favor of settling some issues by vote: Majority decisions form the basis for action in a democracy. Where the concerns of the minority have been expressed and taken into consideration, the loyal support of the minority is normally expected.

*Reaching a Decision or a Conclusion.* What has happened thus far makes it now possible to move toward a decision upon which there will be agreement. If the conclusion is to be really worthwhile it must have been reached after an exploration of the situation and the factors in it which seem important to the group. It must follow a discussion of all the possibilities that are real options, and the reasons for them. It must follow a careful examination of the facts. It must have given full and due consideration to values or points of view that seem desirable to all persons in the group.

In approaching a decision some new alternative may appear. The chairman should never rule out of order a proposal that had been earlier abandoned in whole or in part, or that had not occurred to anyone. The final selection may be a combination of several possibilities. For instance, during a baffling discussion, someone may write out a new proposal which gathers up the conflicting desires in a way satisfying to all. The chairman must be alert, moreover, to the possibility that the group may make a hurried decision in order to end a long session-ignoring many valid points. Sometimes it is wise to take a brief recess, or even postpone final action to the next session to avoid a hasty decision.

The question of the final conclusion should commence with *"what"* and not with *"which."* "Which" means a choice among alternatives already suggested; "what" opens the way for a combination or a new alternative. A conclusion is not necessarily an "either/or"; it may be a "both/and," or it may represent something entirely new that conserves on a higher plane the contribution of all.

How long a group will be willing to postpone decision in order to come to a decision acceptable to all depends on their sense of the importance of the issue and the strength of the bonds that unite them. If the process has been a thorough one, changes will have taken place in the group members individually as progress toward a decision has been made. The situation looks different; the factors important to individual members have been related to factors important to others; possibilities new to individuals in the group have been suggested; knowledge of relevant facts has been gained; new points of view have been examined and individual convictions have been modified. It has been like a chemical process in which the elements are combined in a new pattern, but none lost.

At this point the chairman summarizes the group's decision. "This is what we have agreed upon. . . . Have I reported it correctly?" There is often a noticeable sense of relief, satisfaction, and anticipation in the group, as the summary is made. The leader may wish to express appreciation of the way the group has worked.

*The Practical and Critical Matter of Moving Toward Action.* Too frequently a group stops with the decision that a certain course of action is desired, and makes no practical plans to carry out the conclusion.

It is essential to separate the discussion of ways and means from the determination of what shall be done. Though the practicability of a proposed course of action must be taken into account in the discussion, the claim that it is impracticable must not be used to rule it out. People usually find the ways and means of doing what they really believe in. They have a right to call upon the inventiveness and resourcefulness of the experts in finding ways to carry out their wishes even though the experts may have felt impelled to point out to the group the difficulties of their proposal or questioned its practicability. If in making a budget an organization decides what can be raised before it considers what it wants to do, it will find itself with a very inadequate budget and with less than could be raised. Heroic action and real progress will come only as the ways and means discussion becomes the search for plans for putting into effect conclusions on which all are united. The ways and means committee must be the resourceful servant rather than the pessimistic dictator.

There are several ways of proceeding:

One is for the group as a whole to move right ahead in discovering what practical steps may be taken to carry out the conclusion. In doing so it will use the group thinking process developed above, but now in the narrower area of ways and means.

A second procedure is for the chairman to help the group quickly to identify the various points to be taken care of. (For example, if a trip has been planned, then transportation, supplies, camping equipment are relevant details.) He then assigns these details, and sets a time when the responsible persons will make their proposals to the group. Or, if a group has decided to organize, these items may include constitution, program, dues, and the like.

Or third, if the carrying out of a decision necessarily involves a prolonged period of careful planning, a special committee may be appointed to carry things through to a consummation. This committee has as its basic directive the decision taken by the group. However, it may need to come back to the group from time to time to report progress and to get fresh instructions.

The chairman of this special committee may be the same individual that helped the group make its basic decision, or he may be someone else. In either case the task is primarily *executive,* though extended exploration, deliberation, fact finding may be involved. Much depends on the nature of the original decision. If it was "to build a church at 30th and Euclid," the "ways and means" committee starts almost at scratch. If the original decision included approval of an architect's specifications, the committee is that much further downstream. The group must insist that the method used in putting the conclusions into effect shall be consistent with the values on which they are agreed and shall conserve rather than harm these values. Usually these values are

**40**

points of reference in the ways and means discussion, although sometimes the main underlying questions are considered anew. Practicability becomes a more important factor. The search is for plans which will be effective in carrying out the conclusions of the group.

Now we look at the leader's role more specifically.

# 4

## *the chairman's role in helping groups make decisions*

---

With the chairman rests the responsibility for seeing to it that the conditions for effective group thinking are provided. To conduct a discussion effectively—particularly when it must lead to decision making—requires a point of view and skill. First, let us do a bit of philosophizing about the role of a chairman, president, or leader, in an effort to arrive at a point of view. Then we shall think about the skills involved.

### some philosophizing

*Leadership* is a function in which many or all may share, and the focus of it in any given situation, in any group, is now in this person, now in that one, as each takes the lead in thinking, deciding, planning, and directing action.

The responsibility of the *designated leader* (executive, chairman, coach, director, chief-of-staff) is not primarily to provide directives but to maintain the evocative situation. Though he may be relatively conspicuous, he need not dominate. His role is crucial in keeping the goal in sight, creating a warm and permissive atmosphere for participation, recognizing consensus, helping persons find their parts in cooperative effort, keeping deliberation on the track toward decision.

We measure the effectiveness of the leader not in terms of the leadership he *exercises,* but in terms of the leadership he *evokes;* not in terms of his power over others, but in terms of the power he releases in others; not in terms of the goals he sets up and the directions he gives, but in terms of the goals and plans of action persons work out for themselves with his help; not in terms alone of products and projects completed, but in terms of growth in competence, sense of responsibility, and personal satisfactions among many participants. Under this kind of leadership it is not always clear at any given moment just who is leading, nor is this very important. What is important is that many may learn how to set their teeth into a problem, to apply themselves to it, to work together on it. Leadership of this kind gets more done—more thinking, more action, more final product, and of even greater importance, more enhancement of human values. This point of view with regard to leadership, and the skills in action it requires, are readily learned by most persons.

A person is not born with this skill. He learns it. Some persons with native capacity stumble upon it by trial and error, but, like any other skill, it is learned more effectively by training. If one can study it with others in a group, so much the better. If he does not have this opportunity he can be his own teacher. Fortunately it is not necessary to possess the skill before trying it out, provided the issues are not too serious for a beginner. It is obvious that there are some decisions which have a more far-reaching and urgent impact than others, and that a mistake in group judgment can result in mere inconvenience on one level, dissatisfaction on another, or tragedy where the issues are of the deepest significance.

At any of these levels of decision—from the simple to the profound, from the material to the qualitative and spiritual—the chairman is not usually chosen as an authority, or one who knows the answers. Frequently, and preferably, he is one of the group and is concerned about the questions too. It is fortunate if he knows enough about the members to be able to understand the various reactions they are likely to have, at the same time that he has an open mind which does not try to predict the outcome.

### some useful qualifications in the chairman

1. Know the steps in decision making.
2. Have a reasonably alert mind.
3. Be open-minded and fair, not a protagonist for a point of view.
4. Have poise and self-restraint.
5. Be sufficiently well informed regarding the question under consideration to understand its main issues.
6. Be undisturbed by the expression of strong emotion in the group.

These six qualifications of the chairman are worth the struggle to achieve. They have several values in addition to contributing to the competence of a chairman: they are observed, respected, imitated, and learned by the group members too; and they are qualities that enrich every relationship. They are called qualities of *leadership,* but they are equally useful in situations in which the person, though customarily a leader, is a follower.

#### what the chairman does

*About Mechanical Arrangements.* Whether for a small group, a larger forum, or a great convention, the form and set up of the room are important. A circular seating plan often may give good results in small group discussions. The important thing is that just as far as possible members have a chance to look into the faces of other members. Let them be seated about a table if the group is small. If the group is quite large (twelve to twenty) a hollow square of tables with the group seated on the outside is excellent. An open circle about the room may be convenient. Watch for those who seem to prefer the second row or the corners. Bring them into the main circle if there is room. Participants should be able to take part without rising.

*The Procedure.* The chairman is responsible for procedure. He sees that issues are clearly defined and understood; that the important factors in the situation are brought out and recognized; that the possibilities as to what to do are stated and the real reasons for each seen; that the points of agreement are recognized and the differences understood and explored; that the discussion moves toward an integration of fact and opinion into as united a conclusion as is possible. Then he must see that attention is given to ways and means for putting the decision into effect. In short, he is responsible for keeping the discussion from becoming a miscellaneous consideration of one question after another or an argument with no weighing of fact or opinion.

The chairman gives special care that the discussion

proceeds from point to point. He is alert to the length of time spent in discussing each question, not cutting it off before significant Slinking has occurred, but not allowing it to ramble on and on. In the interest of covering all the points, the chairman does not attempt to push the group forward faster than the development of the thought will warrant. However, it is his business to be on the lookout for the time when enough attention has been given to one section of the group thinking process and the group can move on to the next section.

*Seeking Needed Information.* The chairman will secure information, as far as possible, from the group. Sometimes information is made available through special assignment to particular members of the group. Information can also be provided by persons with special knowledge on certain points who have been invited in. When such persons are used it is wise first to see that they talk in answer to questions which the discussion has raised. There should be opportunity for questions for further understanding of the information. If the chairman has the information, it is in order for him to provide it.

In whatever manner information is secured and introduced, it is the chairman's business to judge the reliability of it and to see that additional facts are secured and introduced if needed.

*Co-operation with the Group.* The chairman will grow accustomed to sensing the attitudes of the group. A group, working earnestly on any question, shows approvals, disapprovals, or differences of opinion quite manifestly. The chairman's success depends upon his learning how to listen to comments and how to watch the facial and other bodily expressions of the members of the group. His acceptance of the members is reflected in their acceptance of him, and this rapport is the basis for good group and leader co-operation.

The spirit or attitude of the session is largely in the hands of the chairman. If he acts as if he were the referee of a fight, then it will have the spirit of a fight. If he pits one side against the other in order to make the discussion lively, he will have a contest on his hands. If he tries to swing the discussion toward his own point of view, and does not give other points of view a chance, he will develop resentment and bad feeling. If, on the other hand, he tries to get all points of view represented, conducts the discussion in the spirit of co-operation, works with the group in finding what is best, then the members of the group will tend to have the same attitudes.

It is sometimes difficult for individuals to raise questions or suggest points of view not popular with the group. The chairman must take care that individuals are not embarrassed in making them, or silenced by sarcasm, wit, or byplay which causes a laugh.

A chairman must have special patience with a new group until it finds itself. They may feel strange, or even suspicious, toward him. They may be strange to each other. They may be strange to the method. They may not be accustomed to discussing things for themselves. By establishing his own honesty and fairness as chairman, preliminary suspicion of him is eliminated, and the group will usually be willing to co-operate with him in finding its own will.

At times, the chairman's co-operation with the group must take the form of calling the wandering discussion back to the point. This does not mean that the chairman is not willing to shift the focus of the discussion, if the group shows its desire to do so. It does mean that if one problem is being discussed and a person wishes to speak on a point irrelevant to the discussion, the chairman as the agent of the group should tactfully rule him out. It is a common habit of some persons not to stick to the point but to use any occasion for making a speech on a particular hobby of their own.

The chairman should, on the one hand, help every person to take part, and, on the other hand, restrain the inveterate talker and keep him from monopolizing the discussion. Just to look encouragingly toward those who are not taking part may be a help. Frequently the expression of the face indicates that a person would like to speak. Recognizing this desire will bring timid ones into the discussion. Sometimes the chairman may call upon certain ones by name. If a person persists in monopolizing the discussion the leader may find it necessary to restrain the talkative member, saying, "Wait a minute, Mr. ——, we want to hear what Mr. —— thinks about this question." This recognizes the value of the inveterate talker's contribution but asks him to postpone his comment until some silent members can be heard from.

It is important for all points of view to be represented. When it is clear to the chairman that something is being overlooked he may see that it is introduced, either by inviting someone especially to do it, or he may do it himself. He may say, "Now I know a person who holds this opinion," and then he presents the point of view of his acquaintance. He asks the group, "What would you say to him, were he present?"

## two illustrations of the way
## in which the chairman may work

The two charts on page 51 are records of two periods in a group leader's training session,[1] in preparation for the small work groups in which a national convention was to be divided. The individuals who were to lead the groups had had some experience, but in previous conventions they had been given detailed instructions, and had been expected to "lead" their groups to certain conclusions supporting the general policies and program of the organization. A change in convention philosophy led to a desire for a change in the way the groups would work.

It was felt by the trainer that some experience with two contrasting leadership roles would be a better way of helping the leaders' group to make its choice of method than just talking about it would be. Therefore, without the knowledge of anyone in the training group (except one individual who kept the record of participation shown in the charts), the trainer used a *directive* role for twenty minutes, as he stood before the group. Then without signal he sat down and, continuing with the session, used an *evocative* role for the next twenty minutes. In both cases the subject matter of the discussion was the work to be done by the group members as convention group leaders.

It may be noted, of course, that the sequence probably favored the success of the second period, because the first period, though formal and somewhat authoritarian, served as a warm-up, to a certain degree. Offsetting this was its effect in creating a mood of willingness to let the leader and the ready talker

---

[1] To make the charts simpler, just half as many group members as there really were are shown here. Letters are substituted for actual names.

**49**

do all the talking. It is quite probable also that in spite of himself, die trainer unconsciously loaded the discussion with his own preference for the second method, though he sought to conceal it. Leaders of discussion can never be wholly unbiased!

Chart A shows the participation pattern in the first half of the leader's session; Chart B, in the second half. As stated above, the periods were of exactly the same length. Several things at once meet the eye: In the second period, participation was much more frequent and, obviously, each person spoke more briefly. The trail of the discussion crisscrosses the group in every direction. In the first half, in addition to the smaller number of participations, the greater length of each one, and the failure of several in the group to participate at all, the lines of participation all radiate from the leader like the ribs of a palm leaf fan. In Period A, the participants kept their eyes on the leader at all times, whereas in Period B they looked at each other most of the time. One of the participants (See F in the charts), in Period A, said nothing. In Period B he became a major focus of the participation. The same was true of Participant C, to a lesser extent.

How did the leader's behavior differ in the two periods? It has been stated that in the first period it was *directive,* in the second, *evocative.* This distinction is apparent in several respects. At the beginning of the first period the leader rose and remained standing. This was a rather natural thing to do in this fairly good-sized group, but it made him the most conspicuous person there. At the end of the first period he sat down and remained seated throughout the second period. In the first period, he directed specific questions to specific persons. He invited questions and, when they were asked, gave

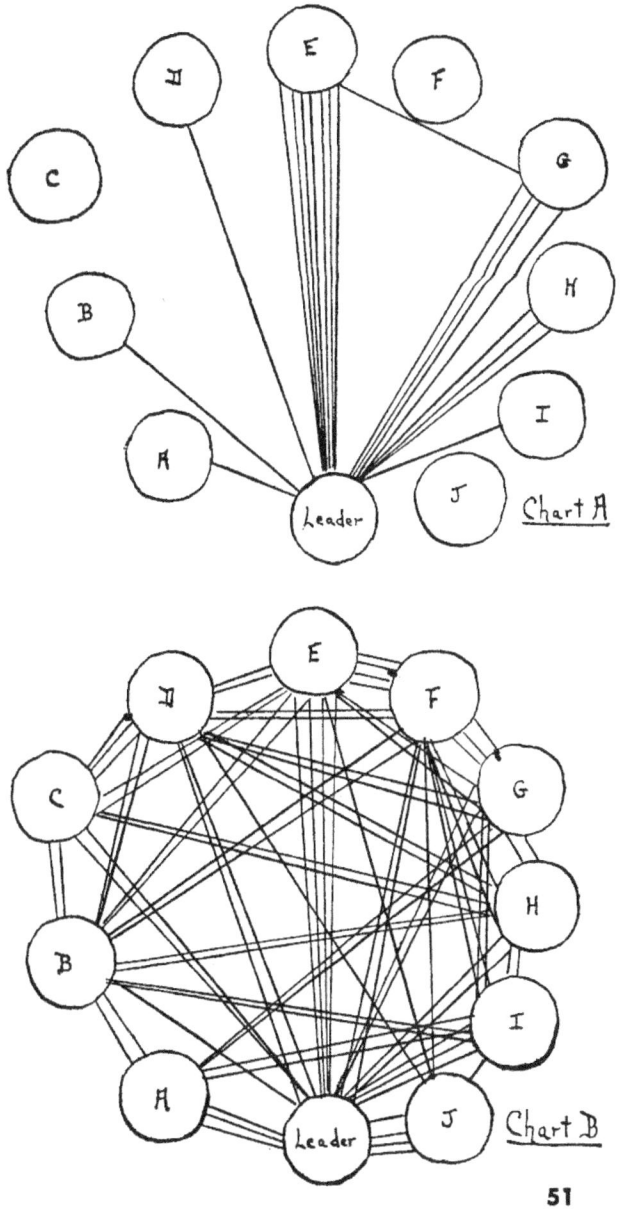

Chart A

Chart B

the answers. He commented on practically every statement made by a participant, either to approve, disapprove, amend, or extend. In the second period, he put questions to the group as a whole and made no comments on statements from participants, but waited for others to speak. His participation (which the chart shows was quite active) was mainly in the following forms: raising questions, such as how to get started, how to get members quickly acquainted; asking for further explanation; asking others in the group to comment; referring questions back (for example, "What do you think?"); silent signals such as a nod of the head to the other side of the table, or to some individual who for any reason might be able to supply needed information (for instance, about seating arrangements, he looked to the general program chairman for the answer); stating consensus (or asking for a straw vote, if consensus was not apparent) on matters that had to be decided; asking such questions as "Is this clear? Do you want to say anything more about this?"; keeping the discussion from wandering (very important); and making summaries from time to time. In Period A, the *leader* was the focus of the discussion, except when some individual might steal the show. In Period B, the *problem* was the focus of discussion, and it was the leader's business to keep it in focus. All the matters that had to be settled in the training session were disposed of by the end of the second period, except one—the method and role of the leaders. This decision came in the evaluation period that followed at once.

In the evaluation session, the group was asked to describe what had happened in terms of leader method, group participation, group interest, and what had been learned—since these were the natural bases on which the work in their own groups would be evaluated. They quickly identified the two phases of the discussion, the differing methods used by the leader, and their differing response in terms of interest and learning. They chose the second procedure, and the trainer spent a few minutes putting its "rules" into orderly shape for their notes, much as has been done in this and the preceding chapter. The group was then shown the two charts of their participation, and they quickly agreed that they felt it to be desirable for the delegates in the convention to have an experience like that shown in Chart B.

### the task of summarizing

The importance of summarizing and, to some extent, its method, has been discussed in Chapter 4. Only a few additional suggestions about the leader's skill in doing it are added here.

The chairman must not summarize too often. To do so means to interfere unduly with the discussion. But he must not summarize too infrequently. At any stage of the discussion where differences or consensus have emerged, and a summary will help to focus the discussion and open the way to move to the next step, he should summarize. Often the next stage is possible because a difference is summarized and discussion focused on a consideration of this difference.

Usually the summarizing can best be done by the chairman. If he finds it too difficult to do this alone, he can ask some other person to co-operate with him by being responsible for it.

It adds to the effectiveness of his summary, either made on the blackboard or verbally, if the chairman keeps it in the language of the group rather than to attempt to make it over into the English of the chairman. Sometimes in response to a summary thus revised a group will comment: "Well, that may be what we said; but it doesn't sound like it!" This is important. Each person must recognize his own contribution.

The chairman must be ready for fundamental modifications in his summary, as the group may desire, and he should not hesitate to adopt changes in the phrasing which seem to the group members more expressive of their thought. He must be careful, however, that this does not resolve itself into a quibble over phrases. Let him, if necessary, state the issue in several ways and come to the place where there is mutual agreement as to the content without an attempt to secure minute agreement on the actual phrasing. A rough summary worked out by the chairman in the midst of the discussion will prepare the way for a more polished statement after the discussion. The success of the chairman in extemporaneous summarizing will be partly in proportion to his experience and practice as a chairman and partly in proportion to his understanding of the problem being discussed.

Summaries must not become exhortations in which the leader gives his viewpoint about what the group has said, or emphasizes the points in the discussion which appeal to him. A summary is simply a reflection of the exact state of affairs in the discussion, and the relating of it to the work to be done. There must be an entire willingness on his part to be an impartial chairman reporting the group's progress, rather than being a protagonist for some point of view.

It must be recognized that a conclusion will not always be reached. If the group has agreed easily, it may mean that it has been doing superficial thinking. If no consensus is reached, it does not follow that the group has failed. The session has been a success if every member sees the problems and its significance more clearly, has been able to look at it from varying points of view and in the light of evidence, and has either come to some conviction or has had his thought processes so thoroughly stimulated that he will ponder on the topic after the group is over.

### the chairman's emotions

The chairman must be careful to keep his emotions from leading him to bias the discussion. If he does feel strongly on a question, his best course of action is to admit to himself and to the group his difficulty by stating his bias and feelings frankly, saying he will attempt to be a fair chairman, but that the group should know his attitude so that it can check him if it thinks his convictions influence his chairmanship. The safeguard of fairness comes in the chairman's trust of the group process.

But a mature and experienced chairman, who is not ordinarily opinionated or biased, may feel disturbed when he sees a group moving toward what he has good reason to regard as an unwise or dangerous or irresponsible decision. What shall he do? When this happens, it is especially important for him to seek to maintain an objective attitude. If the chairman becomes involved in the discussion emotionally he may be the immediate cause of an explosion and it will be fought around him personally. He will have become the center for the divisions of the group and thereby be robbed of any possibility of getting the emotional conflict adjusted. Under these circumstances he will be an unusual person if he does not defend, argue, get angry, and add to the confusion. If he can keep calm and poised, the group may go forward constructively.

Though there is danger that the chairman will interfere too much, sometimes a chairman interferes too little. Thus a leader commented: "I think I could have summarized more without really interfering with the freedom of the discussion. I feel that I asked too few questions. In my extreme desire to make the discussion absolutely theirs, I think I let them wander too much of the time." Fairness and open-mindedness do not mean lack of concern or a *laissez-faire* attitude. cautions to the chairman

Even when a leader seeks to confine himself to a chairman's functions, he may fall into certain faults that hinder the discussion. The most common is for him to take part every time a member of the group speaks. Either he repeats what the group member says or he makes some comment upon it. This is discourteous, it wastes time, and it hinders interest. To break in each time a member of the group takes part means that the discussion becomes one between the chairman and the group rather than a give-and-take among the group members. If the question is worthwhile, the group members may pause and think before they speak. Let the leader be patient and tolerate silence. If no discussion develops in a reasonable time, it is usually because the question is of no significance to the group, in which case the leader should allow the discussion to shift to something of concern.

The chairman's great contribution to discussion is in making it possible for the members to think together. Most chairmen will find this function all they are capable of handling. A useful, and sometimes a surprising, check is to have someone record the number of minutes the leader and the group talk respectively.

To assume, as is often done, that no preparation is necessary for the leading of a discussion is to misunderstand the process itself. The leader must know the "what" as well as the "how" of the discussion he is to lead. He need not be an expert on the subject under consideration, but he must be sufficiently acquainted with the subject and the personnel of the group to see the issues as they arise, to understand the significance of the contribution in the discussion, to make discriminating summaries, and to hold the discussion on the track toward decision making.

In preparing for a group discussion, the chairman must be asking himself: What is the situation? What are our questions? Where do our interests lie? What data will be needed? Many chairmen prepare an agenda sheet on which are listed the items, perhaps in question form, which the group will discuss.

In his preparation he takes into consideration the time and place of the meeting, the characteristics of the setting—good and bad—and factors of time and timing and other interests which some or all of the members may be exploring just before, just after, or right along with the ones on the agenda. Planning cannot be done in a vacuum, and is subject to many possible changes on the spot. The more thorough the preparation, the more flexible it can be when realities demand.

### conviction, prejudice, and values

Annihilation of distance, personal and family mobility, have made our world smaller, but have increased the difficulty of communication. No man can tell the whole truth, for he senses not only with eyes and ears but with his worries, fears, desires, and expectations. Speech may be accompanied by facial expressions and tones of voice that belie it, or may reveal the disputes and conflicts begun in childhood. Experience shows that there is nothing inconsistent with holding a conviction so strongly that one would dedicate his life to it, and yet holding it subject to change. Such conviction is a source of strength in a discussion, but emotional bias may defeat the process. To correct emotional bias is difficult but is one of the group process functions. Where people are not willing or able to examine their convictions and accept the dilemma of choice a question cannot be creatively decided.

And yet on most questions of the day honest and sincere persons disagree, and each course of action may be defended by the same ideals. It helps to admit that most persons have a combination of biased and open-minded attitudes, that none has a right to ask another to reconsider a point of view unless he himself is willing to re-examine his own assumptions. Strong emotion arises whenever there is fear that something will happen to a value that is held dear. When fellowship includes those of different attitudes, experiences, and convictions, it has richness in proportion to the differences. Then there is willingness to give up petty concerns for the good of the organization or the cause, and power is released to be at the command of all those who meet the conditions of spiritual creativity.

# 5

## *special methods in helping groups come to decisions*

---

### visual presentation

Charts may be prepared in advance, or created on the spur of the moment. Data from surveys and other sources are much more provocative when seen as well as heard, and especially when seen in symbols that simplify and stylize the essence of the facts. Slides, filmstrips, and moving pictures can provide often excellent means of setting a good basis for the discussion of the problems they reveal, or of methods they present. Each member of the group should have his own workbook of relevant material.

### brain storming

In brain storming all the members list quickly their ideas about possible courses of action. In this process it is important that no member challenge or censure or even discuss another member's ideas, and the leader himself should guard against making comments other than to encourage responses. When all are in, they can be referred as a package to a committee, or the group can do some on-the-spot classifying of its own. Some ideas can be used for immediate planning—right now, next week, next month; some for long-range planning—next season, next year. Some ideas can be seen as feasible, others not so. Brain storming is especially helpful when seeking alternatives. Knowing that he will not at once be called on to defend his suggestion, a member speaks more freely, and the ideas of the timid often prove to be valid when seen alongside those of the more aggressive.

### buzz groups

This ubiquitous device is a variant of the brain storming technique. If the group contains a dozen or more persons, it is quickly divided into "buzz" groups of about six persons each. Leaders may have been chosen previously, but the more frequent instruction is to ask the person in each group whose last name initial is highest in the alphabet to act as "convener," and the one whose initial is lowest to act as recorder and reporter—or some other equally time-saving device. All the groups may be asked to spend six minutes (or more) proposing as many ideas as they can on the question stated, or a number of questions may be covered by dividing them among die groups. Chairs are pulled into small circles; the general noise of participation doesn't seem to bother; and the leader gives a one-minute warning before calling the general session to order and asking for reports.

### subgroups for more extended discussion

*In a Camp.* An incident occurred that seemed to call for thoughtful consideration and decision by all the campers. The program director gave each cabin leader a brief statement of the problem, together with three or four questions, the last of which was, "What do you think we ought to do about this?" The cabin discussion occurred at bedtime. The results were asked for at breakfast time, cabin by cabin, a boy in each case reporting for his group. The camp director made a summary that the campers approved by vote. The action thus recommended was carried out within twenty-four hours and reported back to the camp. There was general satisfaction.

*In a conference:* "A large gathering has seemed to offer insuperable difficulties to any kind of democratic participation. Hearing is not the only problem involved. This might partially be met by amplifiers with microphones in various places in the hall. A more serious difficulty is that only a few persons can take part in an hour. . . . In a large assembly, the more timid persons are likely to keep quiet altogether and the more aggressive leaders tend to monopolize participation and to give long addresses. Thus a discussional assembly differs from a speaking convention only in that there are a few leaders rather than one, attempting to make up the minds of the many.

"This difficulty has been met by dividing into small sections or groups for discussion and alternating these with general assembly sessions.

"If group thinking is to take place, more is involved than an alternation of group meetings with the large assembly gatherings. The program itself must follow the procedure of group thinking. In order to accomplish this, the conference is planned as a unit, so that the entire gathering in large assembly and group discussions first gives attention to defining the problem, then to consideration of what to do, and finally to ways and means. In such a gathering the platform addresses become resources for the discussion, directly related to the group thinking procedure. . . .

"Each small group becomes really a typical section of the convention as a whole. The large assembly is used for gathering up the results of the small group discussions, for carrying on the discussion in forum fashion, and for hearing addresses on the questions before the groups. The division by types of responsibility is to secure a discussion of ways and means by the groups responsible for carrying the conclusions into practice. . . .

"These delegates will share experience and conviction most effectively if they have had a chance to help decide the program and to discuss the questions before going to the conference. In short, the conference will be most effective if it is a part of the before-conference and after-conference experience of the delegates. It becomes then an item—an exceptionally important item, it is true, but still an item—in die growing experience and responsibilities of the delegates."[3]

role playing

Where a group needs help in looking at things objectively, and in expressing itself honestly instead of saying what members think they ought to think, role playing is a method to enable individuals to discover and express their real feelings. It is the spontaneous acting out of a situation or incident by some members of the group while the rest of them observe. Then the entire group discusses it from two viewpoints: (1) the participants and how they felt, and (2) the observers and what they saw happening. Such an experience often gives unexpected understanding of the nature and strength of the opinions involved, actors and listeners finding themselves free to express themselves. Emotions may be revealed without threat to the discussants, and the emotional content of solutions being considered may in part at least be tested out.

Role playing is another way by which the group may experiment with its own improvement. For example, it may ask a few of its members to hold a short committee session while the others observe. When the entire group then analyzes and diagnoses the session, from the diagnosis may come suggestions about the improvement which the group would like to see.[4]

---

[3] From Harrison Sacket Elliott, *The Process of Group Thinking,* pp₄ 198 ff.
[4] See Alan Klein, *How to Use Role Playing Effectively.*

## *a final reflection*

Again referring to the mechanics, good light, fresh air, a friendly and uninterrupted atmosphere are, of course, all important. But some discussions may start by the pool, or en route to camp on the bus. It takes skill and flexibility to carry the group as far as you can under such circumstances and then pick up at a more auspicious time. For members with no experience to decide to give a coed party can represent a struggle with many more doubts and fears than for a group whose members are used to doing it. A field trip for members used to travel will not be the same as for those leaving the area for the first time.

And so it goes! Ever so often the leader wonders why he does it—all this work and risk, and so many intangibles to consider, techniques to juggle. He has doubts about his own effectiveness: discussion and group thinking can be learned, but has *he* learned them? The chances are that he will never be quite satisfied, but the guarantees are that he will feel a growing satisfaction in the process even if not with his own leadership. If he can say "Yes" to a few of these questions which he asks himself, he may find he is growing better than he had hoped.

- Was there give-and-take? Did we progress from debate to open exchange?
- Did we get some new fight on some old ideas?

- Did I encourage the members' talking in a lively back-and-forth manner, and say very little myself?
- After sufficient exploration did the group make up its own mind?
- Have I become a little less uneasy, a little more relaxed, more confident of the process?
- Shall I take on another assignment? [Of course!]

## *suggested reading*

---

### from this same Leadership Library series

*How to Be a Modern Leader,* Lawrence K. Frank (New York: Association Press [hereafter referred to as AP], 1954)

*How to Develop Better Leaders,* Malcolm and Hulda Knowles (AP, 1955)

*How to Use Role Playing Effectively,* Alan Klein (AP, 1959)

### other books dealing with group leadership

*Committee Common Sense,* Audrey R. and Harleigh B. Trecker (AP, 1954)

*Group Process in Administration,* Harleigh B. Trecker (AP, 1950)

*How to Work with Groups,* Audrey R. and Harleigh B. Trecker (AP, 1952)

*Introduction to Group Dynamics,* Malcolm and Hulda Knowles (AP, 1959)

**Also available from www.sunvillagepublications.com**